The Darkest Time

Michelle Dionne

Presentation by *BookLeaf Publishing*

Web: www.bookleafpub.com

E-mail: info@bookleafpub.com

ISBN: 9789357617925

First edition 2022

To my mom for always believing in me. To Kerra and Kyler for your love and support and to every person who has suffered a loss of any kind. I see you; I love you; I understand you.

ACKNOWLEDGEMENT

I would have never even considered writing this much if it weren't for the honesty shared by my beloved Don on wanting to end our marriage. The pain that it caused was transformed into the words on these pages. Even though our marriage has ended, our friendship will continue. Thank you, Don, for 30 years of learning and growing up together.

PREFACE

These poems were written in the weeks following the end of my 30-year marriage to my high school sweetheart and best friend. The words, emotions and experiences are raw, unadulterated, and harsh. Writing helped heal my heart and allowed me to feel all the anger, grief and sadness that swelled up inside me. As hard as it is to share this very personal journey, I know I am not the only one who has had to navigate these waters. My hope is that someone else going through divorce with a chronic illness will see they are not alone, and that they are loved.

Falling Apart

All is well, or so I thought.
Out of nowhere the information hit me so hard,
my heart shattered.
Hurt, alone, confused.

How will I see light, happiness and hope ever
again?

Tears flowed for days.
Numbness replaced them.
Memories flooded in and the waves of grief
overwhelmed me.

Drowning in sorrow.

Would it be better, easier if it were a death that
was being mourned?
Would it be better, easier to let go of life and
gently slip under the waves of grief and just
disappear?

No purpose, identity lost.
No longer recognize the person in the mirror.
No longer know who I am.

All I know is that there are a million pieces of
my heart scattered on the floor that need to be
put back together again.

The Path

The path looked clear, inviting, safe and true.
There were family, friends, guides, and fellow
travellers too.
It was exciting, hopeful, happy, and fun.
It was a journey I glad I had begun.

The path now has changed, no longer inviting,
safe and clear.
Guides, friends, family, and fellow travellers,
most have disappeared.
It is now a lonely, sad, and depressing place.
It is a journey, alone I must now face.

The path is now filled with twists and turns.
I must go on, as there are no returns.
It is hard, cold and breaks my heart.
It is a journey that I must embark.

The path will guide me to where I belong.
I will be shown that I am strong.
It will bring me back to my soul.
It will help me heal, to be whole.

The path
It is funny that way.

Chronic Illness

Chronic illness is a life sentence.
One of pain, disappointment, and frustration.
Some don't believe you; others feel you are lazy.
And others leave, no longer able to use you in
the same way.

Chronic illness is lonely.
Walking a fine line between staying safe and as
healthy as possible;
And being dangerously close to using up
precious energy;
Or worse, catching something your immune
system can't handle.

Chronic illness is sad.
The life once lived is mourned.
Releasing hopes and dreams from that life
makes the future seems bleak.
What does the future hold? No one knows for
sure.

Chronic illness is a fact of life for many.
It takes courage, strength, and resilience.
Not for the weak of heart, that's for sure.

Shout-out to all who keep moving forward; Your bravery is inspiring!

The day my world fell apart

It happened one day, totally unexpected
My husband, my best friend, my rock, my future
Gone, in one uncomplicated text

My feelings swelled up so intensely I thought I
was having a heart attack
A panic attack is what transpired
Left me gutted for days

The ride has been odd
One moment feeling ok and the next a puddle on
the floor

How could I have been happily married (or so I
thought) one moment and in the next I wasn't?

How is this possible?

Who do I share all my thoughts, feelings, ideas,
and dreams with now?

Depression takes hold
I need help
I am out of sorts in a big way

Pain, agony, grief so deep it carves valleys into
my already fragile heart

It's all happening too fast and too slow.
Let the pain end
Let the new life begin

Healing will take time, energy, and strength
I don't know if I have it in me
My body aches from the chronic pain and
illnesses that already ransack it

How will I go on?
Only time will tell
Only time will hea

The Fairy Tale

The fairy tale is over
No one could believe
The two that should have made it
No longer can achieve

Parting ways is hard
After sharing such a life
Feeling hurt, pain and anguish
From no longer being a wife

Starting over after thirty years
Not knowing what to do
Being alone for the first time
Is something totally new

Figuring out the next steps
And wondering where to go
Realizing all will be ok
That it is time to grow

Becoming

To become a better version
of the one you left behind
is a process worth exploring
it is time to redesign.

Remove the insecurities
the feelings of not enough
delete the thoughts of failure
this will be very tough.

Invite in all the joys
all the experiences you turned down
let people in to love you
yes, they are all around.

There is no end to this growth
and the journey will be hard
the adventure of becoming
may even leave you scarred.

You are worth fighting for
don't let anyone tell you not
keep moving forward in your life
and give it all you got!

Grief

Grief is experienced when something goes away.
It is a feeling that can overwhelm you at all
times of the day.

You never know when it will strike or where you
might be.
But no matter where or when, the pain has
intensity.

Tears may come and pulse may quicken, and
anxiety may soar.
Feelings come forth so quick and painful,
knocking on your door.

Days and weeks and months go by, and grief
still has a hold.
There is no timeline to get over "it", so just
allow it to unfold.

Eventually the pain and anguish don't feel quite
so intense.
The world looks quite different now, your life
ready to re-commence.

Return of the Light

Cracks begin to form in the dark wall that
surrounds you.
Dappled light begins to show.

Perhaps there is hope...
Perhaps joy will return...

Not rushing, not forcing
Allowing the pain, anguish and hurt caused by
the betrayal
to slowly recede into the darkness.

Permitting the much-needed light, love, and
peace
to take its place
slowly infiltrating the dark recesses of the heart.

Unwanted

12

Feeling unwanted by the one that you love has
got to be one of the hardest things to bear.

Giving them your heart, your body, your soul
with promises that were meant to be kept
forever.

Feeling like you are no longer worthy; of not
just their love, but of all love; and the feeling of
despair.

Aching that starts in your heart, that seeps
outward, infecting every cell in your body.

Feeling alone and unsure of where to go, what to
do, or even how to feel.

Words lost, emotions everywhere, body spent.

I AM!

13

I will not throw myself at you.
I am worth more than that.

If you don't want me, that's ok, I will survive.

I love myself enough to leave so I am no longer
subjected to the pain that you cause. My heart,
shattered into a million pieces, will be put back
together again.

I AM worthy!
I AM enough!
I AM loved!
I AM strong!
I AM a survivor!

Feeling

Feeling unwanted
Feeling unloved
Pushed aside
Cast away

Feeling hurt
Feeling abandoned
Heart crushed
Mind overwhelmed

Feeling unappreciated
Feeling uncared for
Forgotten
Alone

Coming Back

15

Shattered pieces of the heart are slowly healing;
Coming back together.

Smiles, laughter, and moments of happiness
happen;
Without even trying.

Catching a glimpse of a person once known;
Aged with the stresses of life.

Fighting, healing, figuring out how to move
forward;
And discovering the identity lost.

Slow and steady progress being made;
A journey of a thousand miles.

Life worth living with a future so bright;
Different, alone, and special.

Light worth shinning for others to see;
Beacon of hope and serenity.

Coming back together to live a beautiful life;
Coming back to me.

A Letter to Chronic Pain

You suck the energy right out of me
You never give me a day off
You force me to abandon plans
And not once have you ever apologized

You prevent me from doing what I love
You keep taking and taking and taking
This relationship is not beneficial in any way
I would like to break-up

Yet no matter what I say, or what I do
You keep sticking around
Creating more pain, more sleepless nights
And more depression

Please go away and give me my life back
Please disappear so that I can wake up in the
morning and not dread the day
Please surrender my body and mind back to me
Please, I am begging you

I miss who I was and what I could be

Me

My Way

You broke me into pieces, my heart, and my soul
I now put myself back together to look and feel
whole

I do so with love, compassion, and care
In a way that makes me stronger, wiser, and rare

I am doing this on my own and without your say
For once I am doing it completely my way

Your opinion no longer matters, and I don't care
what you think
My life is my own now, I finally feel in sync.

The future looks brighter than it once did before
I am excited to go out and experience more

Fear will no longer hold me back
There are mountains to climb and no time to
slack

A new chapter beginning, adventure awaits
My life, my way, as I want to create.

Chronic Illness

Loneliness...
Medications...
Appointments...
Plans left unmade...
Withdrawing...
Alone...
Gaslighting...
Friends gone away...
Bedridden...
Binge watching...
Figuring out what to do next...
Heartbroken...
Relationships Ending...
So hard...
So sad...
So whatever.....................

Questions

Can a broken heart get put back together with all
its pieces back in place or is it more like a puzzle
when missing a piece or is it scrambled up
forever?

Do memories fade like ink on paper over time or
do they burrow into the deep recesses of the
mind only to haunt again later?

Does the body remember the loving touches,
hugs, kisses or is it like a tree building the
outside layer stronger to not feel that again?

Do people pretend to be ok when their world is
falling apart or, do they somehow know that this
falling apart is in fact the experience of falling
into place?

Does the universe play petty games with our
hearts and minds or is it truly a guiding force,
supporting the journey that is meant to be?

I have questions, so many questions....

Colours of the Heart

BLUE when you left me alone after all these years
RED when the anger built up in me like a raging fire
BLACK when I believed all was lost and no potential future lay ahead
YELLOW when a glimpse of hope appeared before me
PINK when I felt inspiration knocking at my door and the creative juices began to flow once more
GREEN when I finally began to feel balanced and grounded
ORANGE when I started to feel confidence return and that I matter to me
BROWN when I began to be honest with myself, my situation, and my life
WHITE when the simplicity began to unfold. No longer needing you and no longer being relied upon.
PURPLE for the return of my spirituality that got lost in the pain, anguish, and sadness, that now offers peace and comfort.
GOLD for the courage to continue the journey on my own and on my terms.

CORAL for the self-love that is so needed.
MAGENTA for the self-compassion that was forgotten.
TURQUOISE for the emotional balance, good luck and friends that offer love and support.

These are the colours of my heart.

Acceptance

Knowing that you can't go back and change the past

Knowing you are worth it to move forward and get on with your life

Knowing that you will be ok because you are loved and supported

Knowing that even though you are drowning in darkness right now, the light will return

Knowing that healing takes time; it is messy; it hurts like hell; and you will be a better version of you once you have gone through the process

Knowing that love still exists; it may look and feel different; but it is there

Knowing that by accepting the present and using the lessons learned from the past, the future is filled with unlimited possibilities

I accept this and am willing to continue the journey

Separation

Life may be different from when we first met
Our hearts have changed, and they still may yet

We grew up together you and I all those years
For that I am grateful, and it brings me to tears

Best friends and then lovers to husband and wife
And now we must go and live our own separate
life

It hurts like hell and my soul will never forget
All the memories made, none that I regret

I do not know what the future holds now that we
have part
But I still love you and always will, you will
forever have my heart

It's going to be OK

Finding yourself is no easy task
It often takes a traumatic experience and
removing the mask

An honest look at oneself is required
Exploring the shadows and allowing them to be
inquired

Uncovering your traumas and acknowledging
the past
Will help set you free to live a life unabashed

Hitting rock bottom, the dark night of the soul
There's so much pain and anguish and the
feeling of losing control

So now there is only one way to go
Forward and up, it is time to grow

No time limit set, no right way to do it
Focus on yourself and you will get through it

The messiness of self-discovery is impossible to
hide

Best you can do is stay focused and continue
with pride

For you are worth the hard journey ahead
Because the world needs you, nothing would do
instead

Keep shinning your light and be who you are
You are loved and cherished, a one in a million
star

The path you travel may never end, so sorry to
say
But remember, it going to be ok.

Feeling Numb

Time has passed since your declaration was said
I no longer feel much
Numbness towards you has taken over my body
and mind

I now see a life without you, alone and being ok
I like what I see
The potential of time and possibilities coming
my way

Decisions, choices, plans; All mine to make
No longer needing approval, discussions, or
consideration

Numbness feels good, better than the chaotic
feeling that took over my entire body, mind, and
soul

I can think a bit more clearly now
I can see a future on my own now
I can taste a new kind of freedom now
I can hear the music of my soul now
I can smell a freshness not there before now
I can feel the old me coming back with new
experiences, upgrades, and outlooks now

I smiled and laughed without you the other day.
At first it felt like I had broken an unspoken pact
with myself to never be happy without you.
Then it felt good, really good
Like I had broken free from the chains of pain,
anguish and grief that were holding me down

I am going to be just fine without you. Maybe
even better!